Agricultural Biotechnology: Risk Analysis Research in the Federal Government

Introduction

The Coordinated Framework for the Regulation of Biotechnology was established by the Office of Science and Technology Policy (OSTP) in 1986 to facilitate coordinated Federal oversight of genetically-engineered biotechnology products (1). The U.S. regulatory policies are based on a scientific understanding of the nature of the products of biotechnology and the best practices for their safe use in general commerce. A rigorous but equitable regulatory infrastructure requires science-based risk analysis and is best served by sound science to inform analyses and decision-making. This is one of the principal tenets of Federal risk assessment research programs and their management and is why such programs have been a part of the research portfolios of several Federal agencies for more than a decade.

The future will likely bring the development of transgenic organisms carrying a host of engineered traits introduced for a range of new purposes; therefore, research priority areas and funding investments can be expected to change as new products are developed. For this and other reasons, the science base for U.S biotechnology regulation is reviewed periodically to ensure that the regulatory infrastructure remains relevant and strong, adapting at a pace sufficient to support an appropriate level of regulation of new products and processes into the future.

Agricultural biotechnology products are defined in this report as plants or animals developed for the purposes of generating human food, animal feed, or fiber. The report focuses on research areas that directly support risk analysis by the Federal agencies charged with regulating agricultural biotechnology products. Risk analysis is defined here to include both risk assessment and risk management. The report focuses on research that supports the regulation of agricultural products currently being commercialized or those soon to be commercialized. Transgenic animals are included as well as plants since these are either currently being commercialized or will soon enter the regulatory process leading to commercialization. The plant traits considered include those most prevalent in current transgenic crops, as well as novel traits. However, while it is acknowledged that pharmaceuticals are being produced by agricultural biotechnology, issues specific to this class of products or related to their medical uses were considered to be outside the scope of the report.

The Agricultural Biotechnology Risk Analysis Research Task Group (AGRA) was formed in 2003 to bring together members of Federal regulatory and research agencies involved in agricultural biotechnology. The charge for AGRA was to evaluate Federally-funded risk analysis research that supports the regulation of agricultural biotechnology products. To this end, it examined the match between agricultural biotechnology research and the needs of the regulatory agencies for research outcomes on which to base regulatory policy. The research needs were identified by the participating regulatory agencies: Environmental Protection Agency (EPA; Office of Research and Development [ORD] and Office of Prevention, Pesticides, and Toxic Substances [OPPTS]), Health and Human Services (HHS; Food and Drug Administration [FDA], Center for Food Safety and Applied Nutrition [CFSAN] and Center for Veterinary Medicine [CVM]) and the U.S. Department of Agriculture (USDA; Animal and Plant Health Inspection Service [APHIS]). The Federal research agencies surveyed were the U.S. Department of Energy (DOE), Department of the Interior (DOI), EPA, HHS/FDA (CFSAN and CVM), HHS (National Institutes of Health [NIH]), National Institute of Standards and Technology (NIST), National Science Foundation (NSF), U.S. Agency for International Development (USAID), and USDA (Agricultural Research Service [ARS], Cooperative State Research, Education, and Extension Services [CSREES], and Economic Research Service [ERS]).

This report presents an overview of a research portfolio analysis conducted by AGRA during 2004 and 2005 covering research supported by the participating Federal agencies for Fiscal Year 2003 (FY 2003). It therefore represents a "snapshot" of the directed biotechnology risk analysis research supported by Federal funding for a specific time period rather than a comprehensive analysis. Consequently, several points should be considered: 1) while the task group attempted to capture all research relevant to the topics of interest, it is possible that some relevant Federal research investments are not included because of inadvertent omissions; 2) the focus of research programs across agencies changes over time and there may be new areas of interest that are not reflected in this report; 3) while this report captures only the research being funded by Federal agencies, there is much relevant research being performed by private companies and non-profit foundations, and; 4) in the time since the analysis of the FY 2003 portfolio was completed, the Federal agencies participating in AGRA have used the outcomes to address risk analysis issues. Coordinated development of new program announcements between agencies and modification of research funding priority areas has already occurred and these activities have impacted the representation of the specific priority areas in the Federal portfolio.

In addition to undertaking the portfolio analysis that culminated in the preparation of this report, the members of AGRA met regularly between 2003 and 2006 to coordinate research activities across the participating Federal agencies. AGRA also organized a well-attended symposium in November 2005 to bring Federal regulatory personnel together with scientists involved in research related to agricultural biotechnology risk analysis. The symposium provided a unique opportunity to enhance the dialog between the two groups and served as an arena for the development of new collaborations and improved coordination of research efforts.

Scope of Federally Funded Research Reviewed

Research related to agricultural biotechnology is supported through extramural and intramural programs across the Federal agencies. Since a basic understanding of bioscience is critical to risk analyses, large portions of Federally-funded research may be relevant to risk analysis of agricultural biotechnology products. Areas of research relevant to risk assessment include environmental science, crop science, agronomy, molecular biology, bioinformatics, genomics and proteomics. The Federal regulatory programs for agricultural biotechnology at USDA/APHIS, HHS/FDA and EPA/OPPTS were used in this report to define research priority areas for risk analysis. In additional, DOI representatives provided input on some of the basic and applied research areas relevant to this agency's regulation of environmental impacts. The research topics covered in the report ranged from broad areas to those focused on specific questions but, where possible, common areas were combined.

Distinguishing between directed and supportive research. As discussed earlier, risk analysis was defined to include risk assessment and risk management. The report divides the relevant research into that directly related to risk analysis of the products of agricultural biotechnology and that supportive of risk analysis. Directed research is considered to deal specifically with risk assessment or management of transgenic plants or animals. Supportive research is related to the research priority areas but does not deal specifically with risk analysis of transgenic plants or animals. Both intramural and extramural research programs were included from each of the participating Federal agencies.

Table 1: Federal funding (FY 2003) of research directly related to agricultural biotechnology risk analysis*.		
Research Area	**Total Funds ($M)**	**Percent Funds by Topic**
Risk Assessment Research		
Total Plant Research	$25.11	80%
Total Animal Research	$2.41	8%
Risk Management Research	$3.89	12%
Total funds* (FY 2003)	$31.41	

*Agencies included: EPA, FDA-CFSAN, USAID, USDA-ARS, USDA-CSREES, USDA-ERS. Programs included: extramural EPA Biotechnology Risk Initiative in FY 2003, USAID Biotechnology and Biodiversity Interface (BBI) grants program in FY01, USDA Biotechnology Risk Assessment Grants (BRAG) program in FY 2003, and intramural USDA Agricultural Research Service (ARS) programs in FY 2003.

Several agencies that fund extramural and/or intramural research directly target agricultural biotechnology priority areas of the regulatory agencies. Such directed research is funded primarily by EPA/ORD, USAID, USDA/ARS, and USDA/CSREES. Examples of specific programs targeted towards risk assessment are the USDA Biotechnology Risk Assessment Grants (BRAG) Program, EPA Biotechnology Risk Assessment Research Program, and the USAID Biotechnology and Biodiversity Interface (BBI) research component. In FY 2003, USDA/ARS funded over 50% of the research directed specifically at agricultural biotechnology risk analysis, including support provided through its internal research programs. Table 1 lists the total FY 2003 support for directed research across the Federal agencies surveyed by AGRA. Specific examples of directed research projects funded by the individual agencies are highlighted in a later section.

As discussed above, supportive research is considered to be any research relevant to risk analysis of the products of agricultural biotechnology but that does not involve transgenic organisms or the direct study of a particular aspect of risk analysis. Agencies such as DOE, DOI, EPA, HHS/FDA, HHS/NIH, NIST, NSF, and USDA/CSREES fund such supportive research. Funded projects cover a broad range of topics, including crop science, agronomy, ecology, molecular biology, bioinformatics, genetics, genomics, proteomics, as well as many other related areas. However, the Federal investment in supportive research relevant to the regulatory research needs was not estimated because the categories are very broad and the scope of relevant research too extensive.

Focus on Risk Analysis Relevant Research

In the discussion below, selected areas of research are highlighted to illustrate the informational needs of the regulatory agencies and how those needs are being met by Federally-funded research. While the research topics identified will inform the risk analysis of agricultural biotechnology products, their inclusion in the report do not imply that there is any inherent risk *per se*. The risk analysis research is divided into three sections: Plant Risk Assessment Research, Animal Risk Assessment Research, and Risk Management Research. In the following discussions, a gene introduced into an organism by genetic engineering is referred to as a "transgene" and the organism into which the gene is introduced as "transgenic."

The bulk of recent Federal funding for agricultural biotechnology risk assessment or risk management research has been in plant-related areas, with only a small percentage of funds going to animal-related research. Therefore, this report contains considerable discussion of transgenic plants and only a limited discussion of transgenic animals, including insects. The regulatory agencies have been handling plant-based biotechnology products for over 15 years, whereas animal biotechnology products are just beginning to reach the commercialization stage. The substantially greater attention to plant-related research is a reflection of the greater number of transgenic plant products coming to market, thus making plant-related risk assessment a higher research priority in the years covered by this report. AGRA is aware that transgenic microbes are used in agricultural applications, for example in biopesticides and fertilizers. They were not included in the current portfolio analysis but may be considered in the future.

In addition, most of the transgenic plant discussion focuses on plant-incorporated protectants (PIPs) and herbicide tolerance, since those are the traits most prevalent in the current transgenic crops. A PIP is defined as a pesticidal activity expressed by a plant and is usually introduced through genetic engineering. However, the use of biotechnologies and their potential products are likely to lead to an even greater variety of transgenic organisms and engineered traits introduced for a range of new purposes. Therefore the research emphasized today will not be the same as that in the next five years and the funding investments will change as new products are developed.

Plant Risk Assessment Research

The future promises the development of transgenic plants with characteristics beyond those now familiar, such as herbicide tolerance and protection against insect and virus damage. The focus of Federally-funded risk assessment research on transgenic plants is for the development of basic, universal or generic principles, rather than to address specific research on proprietary products, so that the outcomes will have the broadest applicability for risk assessment. The work considered in this report has been selected to illustrate how Federally-funded research projects support the regulation of current and near-future agricultural biotechnology products.

For each new transgenic plant intended for commercialization, risk assessments are done on a case-by-case basis, tailored to a specific trait introduced into a particular plant. The paradigms developed for environmental assessment of PIP-containing plants may not be appropriate for other types of trait. However, it is difficult to predict all of the appropriate specific issues and approaches that will be needed to evaluate the types of trait that may be commercialized over the next decade. As transgenic plants with new traits are developed, risk assessors will need to understand the types of effect to be evaluated, from the molecular to the organismal to the ecosystem level.

In FY 2003, the plant-related research topics covered had rather uniform representation across the Federal research portfolio. Overall, the majority of the directed research was being carried out in relatively short-term (2 to 3 year duration) projects by a large number of investigators. Most of the projects in any one area received relatively small amounts of support and were being funded by several agencies. The plant-related risk assessment research area with the largest directed research investment was the potential for unintended biological effects of PIPs. Research areas that represent opportunities for future investment include the potential for invasiveness or weediness of transgenic plants, as well as the development of new methods to assess the potential toxicity and allergenicity of novel proteins added to food or feed through biotechnology.

Toxicology and Allergenicity Studies of Individual Proteins. The diet of man and animals is composed of thousands of different proteins, the vast majority of which pose no food or feed safety concerns. However, some proteins are toxic to humans or animals while others are known to be food allergens (most food allergens are proteins although most proteins are not food allergens). Biotechnology enables the introduction into a food or feed crop of a protein that may not have been previously in the food or feed supply. As part of the data for a safety assessment of such proteins, studies submitted to the regulatory agencies are designed to compare new proteins to the properties of known allergens and toxins. Specific research topics in this area include refinement of computer-assisted homology searches and development of new algorithms to identify potential allergens, investigation of the structural characteristics of food allergens, as well as development of animal models for allergenicity screening of individual proteins. Development of hypoallergenic or non-allergenic plants is also an area of interest.

Unintended Biological Effects of Plant-Incorporated Protectants. The most commonly-used PIPs have been proteins from the soil bacterium *Bacillus thuringiensis* (Bt). Bt spores have been used as a natural insecticide for decades and are regarded as an environmentally-friendly form of pest control. The use of agricultural biotechnology to insert the genes for Bt proteins into crop plants was found to be very effective for protecting transgenic plants from certain insects. However, PIPs may also have unintended consequences for target pest species since selection pressure can lead to increased genetic resistance to a specific PIP. Strategies exist to minimize development of resistance and are in use. In addition, there may be direct or indirect impacts of PIPs on non-target species and ecosystems, including soil ecosystems (microbial, fungal and invertebrate soil communities). Specific research topics in this area include comparison of populations of non-target species co-inhabiting the agricultural ecosystem with biotechnology and non-biotechnology crops, environmental consequences of PIP gene flow into nearby crops, wild relatives, and adjacent natural ecosystems, effects of Bt proteins on soil fauna, efficacy of novel PIP gene combinations, and efficacy of resistance management strategies in minimizing development of resistance, including within-crop refuges. Gene flow is defined as the transfer of genetic material between separate populations.

Areas of Federally-Funded Risk Assessment Research on Transgenic Plants

- Toxicology and Allergenicity Studies of Individual Proteins
- Unintended Biological Effects of Plant-Incorporated Protectants
- Invasiveness and Weediness
- Molecular Impact of Transgenes
- Stable Expression and Persistence of Transgenes
- Genetic Outcrossing in Plants
- Outcrossing Reduction in Plants

Invasiveness and Weediness. Weediness and invasiveness may be viewed as manifestations of competitive advantages that are the result of a complex set of factors interacting in a specific agricultural or unmanaged ecosystem. For the purposes of this report, invasiveness is defined as the competitive success of a non-native plant over native plants when introduced into a natural environment, while weediness is defined agriculturally as the properties of a plant (native or non-native) that interfere with the intended management of an agricultural ecosystem. There is concern that transfer of herbicide tolerance by outcrossing of crop plants with weedy relatives could result in new invasive weeds. Specific research topics in this area include characterization of the factors that determine the invasiveness and weediness of untransformed plants, potential for transfer of herbicide tolerance to related species, and its cost in terms of ecological fitness. An improved understanding is needed of the influence of different classes of introduced traits on fitness and competitiveness, how these vary in a trait-specific and an environment-specific manner, and whether the introduced or transferred engineered traits impact plant communities in positive, negative or neutral ways.

Molecular Impact of Transgenes. Several different kinds of trait have been engineered into plants to date, including herbicide tolerance, virus- and insect- resistance, sterility, and product quality traits. Increased knowledge of the expression of, and interaction between, introduced genes within transgenic organisms will increase the ability to predict unintended effects. Specific research topics in this area include characterization of the stability of, expression of, and interaction between multiple genes introduced into the same plant, comparison of genetic transformation methodologies for insertion-site preferences, insert stability, and any resultant multiple effects from a single gene.

Stable Expression and Persistence of Transgenes. Evaluation of the stable inheritance and expression of transgenes is necessary to determine their efficacy, as well as any unintended effects on the transformed plant itself. Understanding persistence will allow better prediction of potential positive or adverse impacts. The stable persistence of a transgene in the gene pool of a plant population may allow control of diseases such as Chestnut Blight and Dutch Elm Disease. Some factors that may influence transgene stability and therefore persistence include insert location, characteristics of the genetic material inserted, or other aspects of the recipient organism itself. Specific research topics in this area include determination of the stable expression and persistence of transgenes in perennial species, development of methods for evaluating transgene persistence and maintenance of expression, as well as identification of environmental conditions that support transgene persistence.

Genetic Outcrossing in Plants. The potential for transgene transfer, or "gene flow", is an important consideration in risk assessment. However, gene flow itself is not necessarily an adverse event. The potential for hazard associated with transgene transfer should be assessed on a case-by-case basis since it depends on the biology of the plant and the trait involved. Specific research topics in this area are identification of the factors that influence gene transfer rates in self- and out-crossing species, including cross-fertilization of crops by wind, insects, and mechanical devices, determination of the extent of gene flow for some commercial cotton species, and updated measurements of gene flow in current corn varieties.

Outcrossing Reduction in Plants. Baseline biological research on factors that reduce or prevent outcrossing is needed for commodity crops, grasses, and perennials (listed in order of priority). The development of new techniques to reduce or prevent outcrossing would expand the tools available to address agricultural and other environmental concerns. Specific research topics in this area include development of protocols to assess the efficacy of techniques to reduce gene flow, evaluation of biological gene containment procedures (including male sterility), and sterility systems that permit production of non-viable pollen or seeds for wildlife consumption.

The development of commercially-available, transgenic animals is quickly becoming a reality. Risk assessment research on transgenic animals should encompass the potential for impacts on: 1) the health of the transgenic animals themselves, 2) human health, and 3) the environment. For the purposes of this report, animals can be either vertebrates or invertebrates, including mammals, insects, birds and fish.

Areas of Federally-Funded Risk Assessment Research on Transgenic Animals

- Health Effects on Transgenic Animals
- Human Health Issues Associated with Transgenic Animals
- Environmental Impacts of Transgenic Animals

As with plants, transgenic animals are evaluated on a case-by-case basis with regard to the phenotypes conferred on the animals by the specific gene construct introduced and the particular type of animal. The focus of public risk assessment research for transgenic animals, as with transgenic plants, is on basic, universal, or generic principles, rather than specific product characteristics. For example, learning about mechanisms that may drive (or prevent) expression of genes in tissues where they are not normally expressed, as well as identifying and characterizing the components of gene constructs that could promote rearrangements leading to new versions of endogenous pathogens are examples that would be of general applicability.

In animal biotechnology, a basic risk assessment research need is for fundamental information on the biological and ecological interactions of the conventional non-transgenic animal to serve as the baseline understanding against which the effect of the transgenic animal is compared. For example, information on the expression levels of key metabolic markers across breeds, life-stages and environments, and on the health or welfare of domesticated animals is important for comparison of transgenic animals or populations to their non-transgenic counterparts.

Other basic biological and ecological research needed includes understanding the potential for survival of transgenic organisms in the wild and avenues of potentially detrimental competition with native populations. To perform a risk assessment, it is important to be able to characterize the potential hazards and risks for specific scenarios.

The following topics were identified as research areas that will help support the regulation of current and near-future transgenic animal agricultural products. Future transgenic animals are expected to incorporate new traits and different species, so the research priorities are expected to change accordingly.

Health Effects on Transgenic Animals. The potential impacts of introduced transgenes on the transgenic animals themselves can occur at the levels of health and welfare. It is important to know if the insertion of transgenic constructs can have direct and indirect effects on the phenotype of an animal. For example, production of cows that secrete antimicrobial proteins in their milk to prevent mastitis may inadvertently lead to the development of resistant strains of the target pathogens. Specific research topics in this area include archiving of information on the appropriate conventional, non-transgenic animal comparators, including physiological parameters at different life stages of the animals to be modified, key components of milk, meat, eggs, and fiber, surveillance programs for alterations in morbidity or mortality of transgenic animals, and the possibility of gene expression of mammary-intended proteins in non-mammary tissues.

Human Health Issues Associated with Transgenic Animals. Potential human health issues associated with transgenic animals can range from the possibility of toxicity or allergenicity resulting from the consumption of edible products of transgenic animals to the interspecies transfer of biologically-active agents from the transgenic animals to humans (e.g., alteration of host-ranges of viruses or bacteria that are not normally human pathogens, or alterations in the virulence of zoonotic agents (infectious agents that can be transmitted between animals and humans).

Conventionally-bred organisms are also subject to some risks and it is important to understand what these risks are so that that there is a baseline for comparison to any potential risks specifically associated with transgenic organisms. This type of risk could, for example, include altered content of potentially allergenic proteins or susceptibility to disease. Continued research on the potential animal and human health risk issues associated with conventionally (non-transgenic) animals, animal disease agents, disease vectors, and parasites will be essential for making appropriate comparisons with corresponding transgenic animals, determination of the factors leading to production of new disease organisms and assessment of their potential risks to human health. Among the potential risks associated with producing transgenic animals is the possible evolution, escape, or spread of new diseases, particularly viruses that could infect livestock, wildlife, and humans, resulting in economic, environmental, animal, and human health impacts in the United States and other neighboring countries (2).

Specific research topics in this area include identification of potential hazards from different gene constructs, such as mobilization of transgenes to other animals, generation of pathogens with increased virulence or altered host range (i.e., specific organisms a pathogen can infect), generation of novel pathogens, or transfer of drug resistance to pathogens, identification of any potential risks associated with gene stacking (i.e., introduction of two or more genes into the same organism), determination of the ability of transgenic animals to serve as disease reservoirs, and mechanistic studies on the potential production of new disease organisms.

Environmental Impacts of Transgenic Animals. Potential environmental impacts of any given transgenic animal can include those on species coexisting with transgenic animals (e.g., transgenic fish or insects), the spread of biologically active disease agents to non-transgenic species (e.g., generating viruses with altered host-ranges), or the spread of such agents to the air, water, or soil in which these animals live (e.g., altered fecal content impacting soil systems). Specific research topics in this area include characterization of the ecosystem in which the transgenic animals will be maintained, determination of the factors leading to the production of new disease organisms and assessment of their potential risks to the environment, baseline epidemiological research on disease transmission in animals and the potential for transmission to be altered in transgenic animals, development of risk assessment methods for evaluating potential hazards, evaluation of the invasiveness and environmental impacts of mobile and adaptive transgenic species, modeling of fitness factors for transgenic animals and development of sterility mechanisms to provide redundancy to biological confinement.

Research on Risk Management of Agricultural Biotechnology Products

Risk analysis includes not only consideration of the potential for risk through risk assessment, but also the management of risks should they be identified. Research programs are designed to address the scientific bases for developing and optimizing management options whether they are implemented for stewardship of a biotechnology product or imposed through a regulatory agenda to minimize any risk to human health or the environment.

Areas of Federally-Funded Risk Management Research on Transgenic Organisms

- Risk Management and Compliance Verification
- Monitoring Approaches
- Economic Trade-offs and Cost/Benefit Studies

Risk Management and Compliance Verification. Research is needed that will inform compliance verification, such as effective methodologies and technologies for promoting and tracking compliance with regulations concerning transgenic organisms. Specific research topics in this area include validation of the current inspection and compliance standard operating procedures (SOPs), standards development for confinement and containment, development of new technologies to clean transgenic material from planters and combines, testing of new shipping and storage containers for commercial-scale movement of transgenic organisms, techniques for mitigating (or slowing) the development of resistance to insecticidal and herbicidal traits, development of efficient and flexible sampling technologies, improvements in the detection and quantification of transgenic DNA, and the development of tracking methods for transgenic livestock.

Monitoring Approaches. In some cases, it is difficult to predict the ecological consequences of introducing transgenic organisms, including plants, animals and biological control agents. In each instance, it is important to monitor the impacts, positive or negative, as the transgenic organisms are developed and released. Specific research topics in this area include baseline research on the fundamental health of the agro-ecosystem and unmanaged ecosystems, development of methodologies to monitor specific effects of weediness, herbicide tolerance, non-target effects of PIPs, and/or consequences of gene flow, and development of techniques to monitor real-time movement of transgenic material from field tests.

Economic Trade-offs and Cost/Benefit Studies. Economic research aimed at understanding producer response to transgenic products may provide information on the likely rate of adoption and changes in production practices (e.g., reductions or increases in chemical usage). This information is critical to estimating potential ex-ante (prior to commercialization) ecosystem effects and for ex-post (after commercialization) evaluation of policy or regulatory decisions that permit, ease, or facilitate adoption. Broader economic impacts of potential regulatory decisions on producers, consumers, and global markets are helpful in anticipating who will gain and who might lose economic benefits and what market reactions will be upon implementation of regulatory actions. Specific research topics needed to help elucidate the important components in these analyses include examining the factors that determine farmers' adoption of transgenic organisms and the likely extent of adoption of these, as well as measurement of the changes in agronomic practices associated with their adoption such as changes in input use of water and chemicals.

Highlighted Projects from Federally Funded Research

This section provides examples of research projects funded by the individual agencies that are directly targeted to the agricultural biotechnology research needs of the regulatory agencies.

Unintended Biological Effects of Plant-Incorporated Protectants.

The Monarch Butterfly - USDA/ARS

The Monarch butterfly is regarded by many as a beautiful creature so when a report suggested that pollen from genetically-engineered Bt corn might kill Monarch butterfly larvae, scientists from USDA/ARS and numerous universities teamed up to assess the potential risk. The original report showed only that Bt-containing pollen fed directly to Monarch larvae is toxic but did not address exposure in the field. Outcomes from intensive studies suggest several reasons to believe that risk is minimal. Corn pollen does not move very far from cornfields in significant amounts and it tends not to accumulate on the leaves of the milkweed plants that the Monarch larvae actually eat. In addition, the timing of pollen production is offset from the time when the larvae are feeding most actively. These risk assessment studies have contributed to the EPA's decision to continue to allow Bt corn to be grown in the United States.

Managing pest resistance to Bt – USDA/ARS

It has been known since the introduction of dichloro-diphenyl-trichloroethane (DDT) that insect pests can develop resistance to chemical insecticides. Will the Bt trait genetically engineered into crops suffer a same fate? USDA/ARS is monitoring the resistance of cotton insect pests to Bt cotton in order to alert the EPA in the event that resistance begins to occur. USDA/ARS is also conducting research to determine the best management practices to prevent resistance from occurring, with an emphasis on the cotton bollworm. The monitoring has shown no significant change in resistance over the eight years that Bt cotton has been planted commercially, supporting the EPA's decision to extend the registration of Bt cotton for a second five-year period.

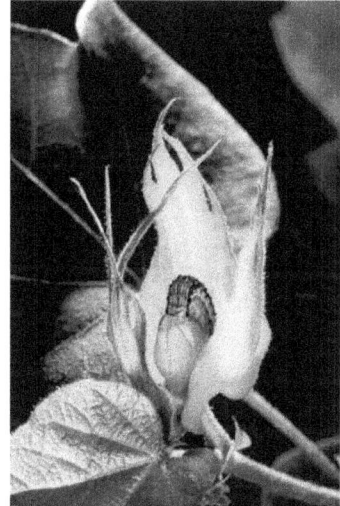

Cotton bollworm eating a boll. (Photo courtesty of USDA/ARS)

Potential impact of biotechnology crops in East Africa – USAID

Outbreaks of pests and disease severely reduce crop yields throughout Africa, hampering efforts to increase access to a safe food supply and to raise incomes. USAID supports the development of biotechnology crops with resistance to some of the most important crop diseases for integration into smallholder agricultural systems (usually farms of fewer than 50 acres). Understanding potential impediments to farmer adoption of new technologies is critical as dissemination strategies are developed. With USAID support, the International Food Policy Research Institute (IFPRI) has conducted case studies for two important food crops in East Africa, cooking banana and corn, to explore factors that may influence the potential impact of biotechnology crops in East Africa.

East Africa is the largest banana-producing and consuming region in Africa. In the highlands, native banana varieties are used for cooking. Farmers use the cooking bananas to feed their families, selling the surplus in burgeoning urban markets for cash. Corn is by far the most important staple food crop in Kenya, which is among the largest producers in Eastern and Southern Africa. Adoption of hybrid corn varieties during the 1960s and 1970s occurred at rates similar to those across the U.S. Corn Belt, but yields in Kenya have stagnated in recent decades. By considering two crops with very different reproductive characteristics, growing practices and markets, the case studies demonstrate the influence that these factors can have on successful technology dissemination, as well as some crosscutting lessons.

IFPRI has combined extensive agricultural production and market information with farmer surveys and geospatial data to capture the diversity of factors that might influence farmers' decisions and simulate farmers' responses to the introduction of a biotechnology variety intended for adoption by smallholder agricultural systems. Analysis of data from field interviews with farmers reveals their perceptions as well as the impediments that must be overcome for widespread adoption of biotechnology products to occur. The analysis estimated the overall potential impact of the technology, as well as the distribution of the impacts across social groups, including consumers.

Photo Removed Due to Copyright Restrictions

Both men and women participate in banana production and sales in Uganda. (Photo courtesty of Bioversity International, formerly International Plant Genetic Resources Institute, IPGRI)

The findings of these studies confirm that smallholder farmers value the crop traits targeted for introduction by current bioengineering efforts. Adoption rates for recently-introduced, conventionally-bred banana varieties with modest levels of disease resistance indicate that farmers would be interested in new transgenic varieties with improved resistance. In some regions of Tanzania, adoption of improved banana varieties has been substantial and farmers continue to seek out resistant varieties, sometimes traveling great distances to obtain them. Although adoption of improved varieties is lower in Uganda, farmers' use of new banana varieties and practices have helped to reduce inefficiency in the production system.

The use of new technology by farmers will expand through investment in innovative means of disseminating planting materials, practices, and information through village associations and social networks. Despite an orientation towards subsistence production,

Photo Removed Due to Copyright Restrictions

In vitro banana propagation. (Photo courtesty of Amanda King, formerly of International Food Policy Research Institute, IFPRI)

the response of farmers to market incentives demonstrate the potential for these crops to generate rural income in local markets. Adoption rates for corn hybrids are already high in the more productive regions of Kenya where commercially-oriented farmers are obvious clients for biotechnology corn. In both cases, the findings indicate that addressing the seed needs of poorer farmers through use of transgenic varieties in more marginal growing areas, where pest and disease pressure is higher, could have a sizable social impact. Industry-wide analysis confirms that in addition to benefiting farmers, improved productivity will benefit consumers through lower and more stable food prices and will add value to other sectors of the economy through linkages with a more efficient staple food sector.

Genetic Outcrossing in Plants.

Gene Flow Research at the NHEERL Western Ecology Division – EPA/ORD

The objectives of the Gene Flow Project at Western Ecology Division (WED) are to develop and validate laboratory, greenhouse, field and modeling methods to assist Federal agency regulatory efforts towards the environmental risk assessment of biotechnology crops. This project includes the use of molecular ecology methods to determine potential exposure of compatible crop and wild relatives to genes from biotechnology crops and possible ecological effects of gene flow on plant communities. The model crops being studied include canola (*Brassica napus*), an annual, primarily insect-pollinated crop and creeping bentgrass (*Agrostis stolonifera*), a perennial, wind-pollinated crop. The results obtained to date indicate that spread of viable creeping bentgrass transgenic pollen can occur at the landscape level, resulting in numerous hybridization events with both crop and wild relatives (3). The current research focus is on the development of methods to determine the potential ecological effects of gene flow on plant communities in non-agronomic ecosystems.

Field studies constitue an important part of ecological risk asssessment of the safety of transgenic crops. A researcher from EPA/NHEERL/WED is preparing to place a pot of non-transgenic creeping bentgrass in position in a non-agronomic area of central Oregon as a sentinel plant; i.e., to determine if it will become hybridized by pollen from experimental fields of transgenic creeping bentgrass. (Photo courtesty of EPA)

Isolation and characterization of DNA from plant samples constitutes an important part of the research carried out by the EPA/NHEERL/WED Ecologicial Effects of Gene Flow project team. This photo depicts a researcher collecting plant material from which DNA extracts will be prepared for molecular characterization. (Photo courtesty of EPA)

Quantifying Aerial Dispersal of Corn Pollen – USDA/CSREES

Aerial movement of corn pollen is problematic for those seeking to maintain genetic purity during seed production or to preclude unintended movement of transgenes into food or feed corn. Dr. Don Aylor (Connecticut Agricultural Experiment Station, New Haven) is using remote-control model aircraft to sample air at varying levels above the corn crop canopy and ground-based samplers for within-canopy measurements of pollen content. The model takes into account the ability of pollen to germinate (survive) after dispersal, various atmospheric factors, and corn silk and pollen geometry to assist prediction of the likelihood of pollen deposition and hybridization with a receptive plant. This study should provide regulators with a more accurate and realistic model to describe corn pollen movement away from a field and thus to set isolation distances for segregating corn lines. The final model will allow for predictions of pollen movement over distances of less than one meter to over ten kilometers.

Photo Removed Due to Copyright Restrictions

Corn anthers shedding pollen. (Photo courtesty of Don Aylor, Connecticut Agricultural Experiment Station, New Haven)

Enhancing the Safety of Transgenic Bahiagrass – USDA/CSREES

Bahiagrass (*Paspalum notatum*) is the most widely-grown forage grass in Georgia, Alabama and Florida, and is also cultivated as a turf or utility grass. Pollen production could lead to the unintended spread of transgenes, so Dr. Fredy Altpeter (University of Florida, Gainesville) is determining the extent of pollen-driven gene flow in this grass, as well as developing methods to prevent transgene movement. One possible approach is to create male-sterile plants that do not produce viable pollen. Insertion of the transgenes into the choloroplast genome is also being explored to prevent transgene movement through pollen, since chloroplast genes are generally inherited maternally.

Photo Removed Due to Copyright Restrictions

Bahiagrass is a popular forage grass in the southeastern U.S. (Photo courtesty of Freddy Altpeter, University of Florida, Gainesville)

Coupling Lagrangian Stochastics with Large Eddy Simulation to Predict Corn Pollen Dispersal – USDA/ CSREES

Dr. Mark Westgate (Iowa State University, Ames) is studying the production and movement of corn pollen under the corn growing conditions typical of the Midwestern U.S. This is the first time that a study of the production and dispersal of transgenic pollen has been coupled with a prediction of out-crossing to an adjacent field. Westgate and colleagues used a particle dispersion model to predict the pattern of pollen flow from genetically-engineered corn to adjacent fields of non-transgenic corn. Particle dispersion models compute pathways for a large number of individual particles (pollen in this case) to describe the transport and diffusion of substances in the atmosphere. The researchers' results clearly demonstrate that potential for gene flow in corn can be assessed from the flowering dynamics of the crop. They also confirmed that this approach for predicting pollen dispersal provides a fairly accurate profile of pollen deposition for up to about 300 meters from the pollen source. Movement of pollen is a critical metric in instances where genetic purity of breeding lines is required and in cases involving experimental use permits.

Photo Removed Due to Copyright Restrictions

Stamens of the corn male flower (tassel) shed pollen. (Photo courtesy of Wikipedia, GNU Free Documentation License)

Environmental Impacts of Transgenic Animals.

A Model for Assessing Ecological Risks of Transgenics – USDA/CSREES

Researchers at Purdue University and the University of Minnesota have developed and tested a "net fitness" model to assess the potential ecological impacts of transgenic fish. The net fitness approach looks at factors related to the viability and the ability to reproduce of transgenic organisms compared to the non-transgenic relative. The model includes six fitness factors: juvenile viability, female fecundity, male fertility, mating success, age to sexual maturity, and adult longevity. With these six factors, the model can theoretically predict the effect on population growth and transgene spread of transgenic organisms released into the environment. The model is available as an optional risk assessment tool for regulatory agencies and developers of transgenic organisms.

In 2003, participants in a workshop held in Colorado Springs examined the possibility of extending this type of net fitness model from the spread of transgenes in fish to gene flow in crop plants. The workshop participants noted that the direction of evolution for a transgene entering a wild population is influenced by the genetic backgrounds into which the transgene is introduced and by changes in net fitness as a result of natural selection on that genetic background. Predicting the outcomes of natural selection is a two-step process involving (1) estimation of net fitness components for alternative genotypes, and (2) incorporation of parameters into a model that predicts change in gene frequency and population size.

It was recognized that alternative scenarios and methodologies (for example, crop-to-crop outcrossing) should be considered in the comprehensive evaluation of potential risks posed by deployment of a transgenic crop. The workshop discussions centered on improvements to the model, as well as recommendations for testing the model. The workshop report is available at *http://www.isb.vt.edu/news/2004/news04.Jan.html.*

Biological Containment of Genetically Engineered Fish – USDA/CSREES
Dr. Alison Van Eenennaam (University of California, Davis) is addressing the need for containment of genetically-engineered fish, such as salmon, that are currently going through the regulatory review process. As commercially-important fish with enhanced traits come closer to market, there is a need to address the potential for escape or release of these fish into wild populations. Dr. Van Eenennaam's work focuses on the use of site-specific recombinases to prevent the transfer of genetically-engineered DNA to wild populations of sexually-compatible fish through mating. Dr. Van Eenennaam and her colleagues are using the zebrafish (*Danio rerio*) as a model for studying different methods for the reproductive containment of transgenic fish. They plan to determine the feasibility of containing transgenic DNA by using a promoter active only in the germ-line of the organism to drive a recombinase capable of recognizing specific, short DNA segments engineered into the fish. This will cause the excision of the transgene from the gametes (sperm and eggs), while still retaining the advantageous effects of the transgene in all the other parts of the fish. This approach will prevent transgene transfer even if mating were to occur among escaped fish and native populations.

Photo Removed Due to Copyright Restrictions

Zebrafish is a good model to test for the spatial expression patterns conferred by a promoter. For example, the red fluorescent marker (DsRed-Express) clearly labels genes expressed in the gonad. (Photo courtesty of Bruce Draper, University of California, Davis)

Conclusions

The AGRA task group has provided an important forum for members of Federal regulatory agencies, the Federal agencies that conduct and fund agricultural biotechnology research and the broader community to discuss those areas of research that are necessary to maintain the U.S. government's strong scientific basis for agricultural biotechnology risk analysis. It also provided an opportunity for Federal government agencies supporting other types of research to provide feedback on the risk assessment discussion and valuable access to research organizations not typically contacted by the regulatory agencies. Many of these topic areas are especially important for the supportive research discussed in this report.

The members of the AGRA task group examined the scientific foundation for the risk assessment undertaken by the Federal government and identified information areas that could be improved or made more complete. These particular areas of interest, while essential to risk assessment, are often overlooked by academic and Federal researchers intent on publishing ground-breaking innovations. These specific areas include baseline data on the composition of foods including animal products, monitoring for ecosystem effects, functional features used to identify weediness and invasiveness, and pollen biology in relation to plant outcrossing. These topic areas are broader and longer-term than those encompassed by most targeted research programs.

The role of Federally-funded research is critical because it deals with issues of long-term public benefit that cannot as easily be addressed by private, for-profit companies. Federal research that is funded independent of commercial interests can also provide the level of credibility and transparency necessary to achieve and maintain public trust and confidence in the regulatory system. This role, which includes directed research for the Federal regulatory agencies, must be focused and strengthened to maximize impact and maintain the efficacy of the Federal regulatory system.

For Federally-funded research to be most effective, sustained coordination is needed among Federal agencies. Since research related to the risk analysis of the products of agricultural biotechnology is being supported by several agencies, coordination ensures that all of the diverse research areas of need are covered and that the data are communicated to the regulatory agencies. The AGRA task group has demonstrated that collaboration between and coordination among Federal agencies can be achieved through an interagency task group. The activities of the AGRA task group have already had an impact on Federally-funded research portfolios through coordinated agency input into program announcements. In addition, the AGRA-sponsored symposium bringing together representatives from Federal agencies with academic researchers was extremely valuable for fostering communication between these two communities.

Coordination of Federal agencies in this arena will continue through the Agricultural Biotechnology Working Group, which is co-chaired by OSTP and the National Economic Council and includes representatives from USDA APHIS, EPA, and FDA with regulatory responsibilities for agricultural biotechnology. Agency coordination through this working group will ensure that regulation keeps pace with changing technologies and that there continues to be a strong scientific basis for agricultural biotechnology regulation in the United States.

References

1. Coordinated Framework for Regulation of Biotechnology, June 26, 1986, Federal Register 51:23302.
2. Animal Biotechnology: Science Based Concerns, 2002, National Academies Press.
3. Watrud et al., 2004, PNAS 101:14533-14538

Acknowledgements

The current members of the AGRA Task Group express their appreciation for the efforts of the following former members and participants who were instrumental in preparing this report:

Stefi A. Baum (formerly DOS)
Jack Bobo (DOS)
Mary Bohman (USDA)
Susan J. Carlson (USDA, formerly HHS/FDA)
Clifford J. Gabriel (EPA, formerly OSTP)
Indur Goklany (DOI)
Debra Hamernik (USDA)
Josette Lewis (USAID)
T. Clint Nesbitt (USDA)
Larisa Rudenko (HHS/FDA)
Kurt Zuelke (USDA, formerly OSTP)

Abbreviations

APHIS:	Animal and Plant Health Inspection Service
ARS:	Agricultural Research Service
BBI:	Biotechnology and Biodiversity Interface
BRAG:	Biotechnology Risk Assessment Grants
CFSAN:	Center for Food Safety and Applied Nutrition
CSREES:	Cooperative State Research, Education, and Extension Services
CVM:	Center for Veterinary Medicine
DDT:	Dichloro-diphenyl-trichloroethane
DOE:	Department of Energy
DOI:	Department of the Interior
EPA:	Environmental Protection Agency
ERS:	Economic Research Service
FDA:	Food and Drug Administration
HHS:	Health and Human Services
IFPRI:	International Food Policy Research Institute
NHEERL:	National Health and Environmental Effects Research Laboratory
NIH:	National Institutes of Health
NIST:	National Institute of Standards and Technology
NSF:	National Science Foundation
OPPTS:	Office of Prevention, Pesticides, and Toxic Substances
ORD:	Office of Research and Development
OSTP:	Office of Science and Technology Policy
PIP:	Plant-Incorporated Protectant
SOP:	Standard Operating Procedure
USAID:	U.S. Agency for International Development
USDA:	U.S. Department of Agriculture
USGS:	U.S. Geological Survey
WED:	Western Ecology Division